A NOTE TO PARENTS

Learning to recognize feelings and finding appropriate ways to express them are important steps in any child's growth. Pretending can be a big help to children as they work to understand more about feelings, but grownups sometimes need to clarify for children just where pretend stops and reality begins. That's one reason why, in both our storybooks and television programs, we keep the Neighborhood of Make-Believe separate from our "real" neighborhood. In Make-Believe, we pretend about certain things that couldn't happen in real life...and make it clear that that's what we're doing.

Each book in this series tells a story about feelings. Some of those feelings are happy ones and some aren't—jealousy and anger, for instance. Strong feelings can be hard to talk about, but pretending about them can make it easier. We hope that these stories will help you talk about feelings in *your* family. Though the stories are only make-believe, the feelings are real, and children need to know that having feelings of all kinds is a very real part of what makes us human beings.

Fred Rogers

Library of Congress Cataloging-in-Publication Data:
Rogers, Fred.   If we were all the same.
SUMMARY: Tired of looking exactly alike, the people of the purple planet decide to become more colorful.   [1. Individuality—Fiction.
2. Color—Fiction] I. Sustendal, Pat, ill.   II. Mister Rogers' neighborhood (Television program)   III. Title.   PZ7.R63If   1987   [E]   86-31598
ISBN: 0-394-88778-6 (trade); 0-394-98778-0 (lib. bdg.)

Manufactured in the United States of America   1 2 3 4 5 6 7 8 9 0

A STORY FROM

If We Were All the Same

By Fred Rogers

Illustrated by Pat Sustendal

Random House 🏠 New York

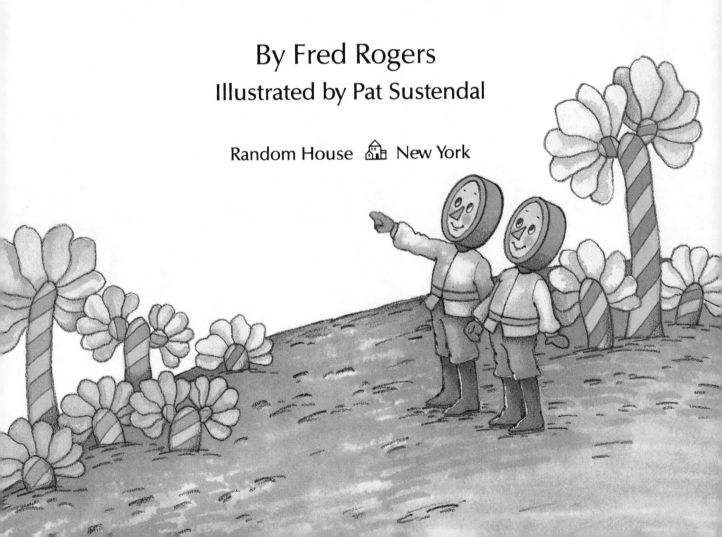

Suppose everyone in the world looked exactly the same—everyone ate the same food, lived in houses that were the same, and even had the same thoughts.

How do you think it would feel to be in a world like that?

We could make up a story about that. Pretending things is often a good way to find out how you feel about them. Let's make it a story about the Neighborhood of Make-Believe. *Anything* can happen there!

Ready, Trolley? Let's go!

Let's pretend that Lady Elaine Fairchilde is flying on her very own spaceship.

She had been out to visit the stars and was on her way home again, when suddenly she saw a purple something floating in the sky.

"That's out of this world!" she said to herself. "I'd better go right over and take a look!"

The purple something turned out to be a tiny
purple planet. When Lady Elaine landed there, she knew
at once she was in a very strange place.

Everything was purple! The sky was purple. The grass
was purple. The trees were purple. The people were
purple.

Not only was everything purple, everything was exactly
the same. The cars were all the same. The houses were
all the same. The people were all the same. Everybody
talked the same and walked the same. Everybody even had
the same ideas.

What's more, the only animals on Planet Purple were
purple pandas—and they were all exactly the same too.

When Lady Elaine stepped off her spaceship, she saw two purple people and a purple panda right away.

"Toot! Toot!" she said. "I'm Lady Elaine Fairchilde from the Neighborhood of Make-Believe. Who are you?"

"I am Paul," said one of the purple people.

"I am Pauline," said the other purple person.

"I am Purple Panda," said the panda.

"And where in the world are we?" Lady Elaine asked.

All together, in the same kind of voice, they answered, "You have discovered Planet Purple!"

"Whoopee!" shouted Lady Elaine, and she took a good look around. To her surprise she found out that Planet Purple people even had the same names. Every man was called Paul. Every woman was called Pauline. Every panda was called Purple Panda.

The purple people were surprised too. The first time they'd seen the color green was when Lady Elaine's spaceship landed from the purple sky.

They were certainly surprised to meet a pink person.

"Just wait till I tell the folks back home about this place!" Lady Elaine said.

As soon as Lady Elaine took off again for home,
Paul and Pauline and Purple Panda had a new idea.
It was the first new idea on Planet Purple. "Someday soon,"
they decided, "we will go visit this strange person from the
Neighborhood of Make-Believe."

When her spaceship landed at home, Lady Elaine hopped out and told everyone about Planet Purple. She even talked about it on television.

"It's a great place," she said, "and *I* discovered it! From now on, we're going to do things the Planet Purple way around here!"

Lady Elaine did everything she could to be just like the people on Planet Purple. First, she painted all the rooms in the Museum-Go-Round purple.

Next, she ordered some purple clothes.
Then she started to eat only purple
pumpernickel pudding.

And she insisted that everyone be
called Paul or Pauline. And, of course,
she called herself Pauline.

One morning Lady Elaine woke up to find she had visitors from Planet Purple: Paul, Pauline, and Purple Panda. "We traveled the purple way," they explained. "All we had to do was think of being here with you—and here we are!"

The Planet Purple visitors could hardly believe what they saw. Everything in *this* neighborhood was different! The sky was blue. The grass was green. The houses had different shapes. No one looked exactly the same.

Lady Elaine took the visitors to the castle to introduce them to the queen and king.

"This is Queen Pauline and King Paul," Lady Elaine explained to her new friends.

"It is a pleasure to welcome such distinguished guests," said the king. "However, Lady Elaine, my name is King Friday XIII and this is Queen Sara Saturday, as you well know!"

"That's what you think," said Lady Elaine. "You're Paul and she's Pauline to me! And you can call me Pauline, too, while you're at it!"

The visitors looked nervous. "That is a strange way to talk to a king," said Purple Panda.

Queen Sara smiled. "That's all right, Purple Panda," she said. "Lady Elaine often has ideas of her own. If we were all the same, our kingdom would be a lot less interesting. That's one reason Lady Elaine is so important to us."

"Lady Elaine Fairchilde is important to us on our planet, too," Paul and Pauline said.

"Well, what d'ya know about that!" said Lady Elaine.

Paul and Pauline liked the Neighborhood of Make-Believe. Before they went home, they did as much exploring as they could.

Purple Panda was so excited with all the new and different things that he decided to stay there.

Before Paul and Pauline went home, they looked and they listened, and they smelled and they touched. They spent their time collecting different colors and sounds, smells and feelings.

One day Paul was outside the castle trying to gallop like a horse. Suddenly he tripped and fell and hurt his knee. Then the strangest thing happened. Something wet started coming down his cheek.

"Are you all right, Paul?" asked Queen Sara, who happened to be walking in the garden.

Paul rubbed his knee. "I think so," he said. "But what is this water coming from my eyes?"

"That's called tears," said Queen Sara, sitting down beside him, "and when tears come down your face, that's called crying. It's one way we have here for telling people we need them."

When Pauline saw Paul's tears, she put her arms around him. Queen Sara smiled. Paul felt better. "I never knew I could feel so many different ways," said Paul.

He and Pauline could hardly wait to tell their purple friends about all the different things in the Neighborhood of Make-Believe. So they just thought about being back on Planet Purple...and thought again... and all at once that's exactly where they were.

Paul and Pauline told all their Planet Purple friends about the Neighborhood of Make-Believe. "Everything is so different, and nobody is exactly the same as anyone else," Pauline explained. They talked about the color of a clear blue sky, the sound of a yellow canary, the smell of a green mint leaf, and the taste of a red tomato. Paul told about crying, and all the different ways of feeling. The people on Planet Purple liked what they heard.

"But where is Purple Panda?" asked the other purple pandas.

"He decided to stay in the Neighborhood of Make-Believe," said Paul. "He liked being the only purple panda there."

"But I miss Purple Panda and I want to see him again," said Purple Panda's best friend, blinking his eyes. A few tears ran down his cheeks. That was the very first time anyone on Planet Purple had felt sad.

"Purple Panda will be back to visit," said Paul, giving the sad panda a hug.

The people on Planet Purple decided to make some changes. Someone wanted to live in a blue house and another wanted to live in a yellow house. Some people started wearing red clothes and eating green food. Before long, everyone on Planet Purple began to walk and talk in different ways. They no longer wanted to be exactly the same!

And even though Purple Panda remained in the Neighborhood of Make-Believe, he sent messages to all his friends back home, and they sent messages to him.

"Well, what's the news from the old purple planet?" asked Lady Elaine one day.

"Things are changing there," Purple Panda told her. "Now everyone likes being different. And it is all because of you. You showed us what *different* is."

"I did?" said Lady Elaine. "Little ol' me?"

"Yes," said Purple Panda, "and we have even changed the name of our planet. It is now called Planet Purple Fairchilde in your honor."

"Whoopee!" shouted Lady Elaine. "Fairchilde's the name and discovery's the game! Wait till I tell King Paul—"

"Lady Elaine—" interrupted Purple Panda, looking nervous again.

"Oh, all right," said Lady Elaine. "Wait till I tell King Friday. Come to think of it, I guess I'm glad Friday's just who he is too."

And she and Purple Panda made plans to visit Planet Purple Fairchilde to celebrate many different things.

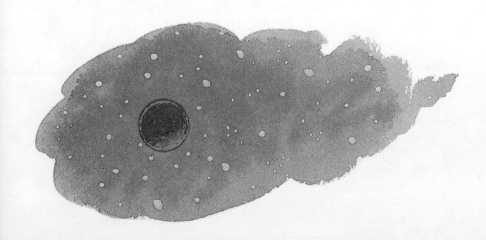

Isn't it good to know that we can have some things that are the same and some things that are different no matter who we are? Nobody has to be exactly like anybody else, but people can like us exactly as we are.